Thanks to Emily, my mother, and all my family for encouraging me.
Thanks to Roger for his help, and to Emeka for inspiring me.

A is for AFRICA © Frances Lincoln Limited 1993
Text and illustrations © Ifeoma Onyefulu 1993

First published in Great Britain in 1993 by
Frances Lincoln Limited, 4 Torriano Mews,
Torriano Avenue, London NW5 2RZ

British Library Cataloguing in Publication Data
available on request

ISBN 0-7112-0848-4

Set in Newtext ITC Book
Printed and bound in Hong Kong

Designed by Patricia Howes

The endpapers are based on a textile design by Chinye Onyefulu.

5 7 9 8 6

A is for AFRICA

An alphabet in words and pictures

Ifeoma Onyefulu

FRANCES LINCOLN

Author's note

This alphabet is based on my own favourite images of the Africa I know. I come from the Igbo tribe and grew up in south-eastern Nigeria. It was in Nigeria that these photographs were taken, but the people and things pictured reflect the rich diversity of the continent as a whole. There are examples of Moslem and Arabic influences drawn from the north of my country, as well as costumes and ornaments from the south, where the religions are animist or Christian. There are kola nuts, indigo and beaded jewellery to show something of the variety of Africa's wealth. And though other Africans may use a different kind of nut, a different colour dye and jewellery that looks different, the meanings and customs associated with them are the same.

However, I wanted to capture what the people of Africa have in common, too: traditional village life, warm family ties – and above all the hospitality for which Africans are famous.

This book shows what Africa is to me, but it is for and about all the peoples of this vast, friendly, colourful continent.

is for Africa, a great continent of many countries and peoples. The African people come from large families called tribes. They may dress differently and speak different languages, but Africa is home to them all.

Bb

is for the Beads a girl may wear on her head, ears, or neck. They come in lots of different shapes, sizes and colours - red, green, blue and yellow.

is for Canoe, to paddle down the river. Canoes are used for fishing and carrying goods to market. People may visit their friends or take their children to school by canoe.

Dd is for the Drums used to make music and announce special meetings and important news in many villages. When a newborn baby is named, relatives and friends may welcome him or her into the world with the sound of drums.

Ee is the Embrace we give our loved ones. Africans are very warm people, and this is how they welcome relatives and friends. Dancers embrace at the end of a performance. They embrace to show their happiness and give each other support.

Ff is for the Feathers an Igbo chief wears on his hat. Hats and feathers are handed down from father to son, when the son reaches middle age. This Igbo chief's feathers are from the eagle. In this tribe, women can be chiefs too, but they don't wear feathers.

is for Grandmother, telling wonderful stories about animals and people who lived long ago. She is a very special person in family life.

Hh

is for mud Houses, just right for a hot climate. Most places in Africa are hot during the day and cool at night. In the daytime, the mud walls keep out the hot sunshine. At night, the mud bricks release the heat they have absorbed during the day and warm the inside of the house.

is for Indigo, a blue powder that comes from the indigo plant, which is used to dye clothes. A good way to dye cloth is to leave it to soak in a mixture of powder and water in a very deep hole in the ground. Letting the cloth dry in the open air helps set the colour.

is for Jumping with the other children in the village. In the evenings when the sun is setting, children gather to play. Jumping over a stick is a favourite game.

Kk

is for the Kola nuts offered to guests to show warmth and friendship in many parts of Africa. On an important occasion, old men and women may say prayers and the oldest man present breaks the kola nuts. The nuts grow in pods on tall trees, and they keep well after they have been picked.

Ll

is for Lamps. Some home-made lamps are made of clay, but these are used milk-tins. They have wicks to burn oil, paraffin or kerosene.

Mm

is for Masquerade, a mask and costume made to honour the spirit of an ancestor. They are sacred objects, brought out only for special occasions. The artists chosen to make masquerades spend months designing them before they show them in public.

is for Neighbours, passing on the latest news.

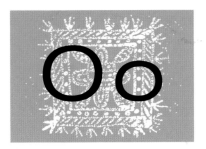

Oo

is for Ornaments to adorn
our bodies. African people
love to dress up and look
beautiful. In some tribes
people wear decorated
bands around their waists
or across their chests.
Body markings are
another kind of ornament.

Pp is for earthenware Pots, for storing water and keeping it cool. They give the water a fresh, earthy taste. Women sometimes use a pot as a musical instrument, beating it to give out a very deep sound.

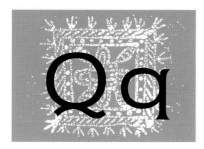

Qq

is for Queen, wearing her crown and splendid jewellery. Not so long ago, there were lots of powerful kings and queens in Africa, but nowadays there are only a few.

is for River. Africans believe many rivers are sacred. In villages they take care to keep their river clean, and people set aside special areas for fishing, washing and swimming.

is for Shaking hands. Children and grown-ups shake hands when they meet friends or relatives. When two Igbo chiefs shake hands they use the back of the hand, not the front, to show how important they are. Young men and women raise and clasp hands with their friends at big gatherings.

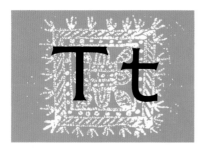

Tt

is for Turban. A Muslim man may wear this special turban if he is very knowledgeable about the Islamic religion and after he has visited Mecca (the holy centre of Islam). Women may also wear turbans to help them carry heavy loads on their heads.

Uu is for Umbrella, even better than a big leaf for giving shelter from the hot sun. A mother will use an umbrella to shade a new baby, and market traders will use one to stop their goods wilting in the sun.

is for the Village, where many people live together, sharing the same traditions and beliefs. The old people in the village teach the young ones the old customs, as they were once taught themselves.

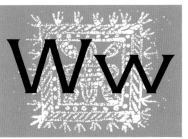 is for Weaving. Some tribes weave their own fabrics from locally-produced cotton. Parents teach the craft to their children. Each region has its own story of how weaving began.

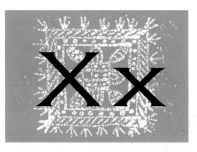

is for the Xylophone many villages use in their music. It is made from wood that gives a beautiful sound. Each key is a different length and makes a different note when the player strikes it.

is for the Yams that grow in our gardens. They are like potatoes, but yams are bigger and take longer to grow. We boil yams or roast them and eat them with palm oil. Either way, they taste delicious!

is the rough Zig-zag lane leading to my village.
And that's the end.